How to Burn Down the House

How to BURN DOWN the HOUSE

the infamous waiter & bartender's SCAM BIBLE

by

TWO BOURBON STREET WAITERS

PETER FRANCIS & R. CHIP DEGLINKTA

New Orleans

How to BURN DOWN the HOUSE

the infamous Walter & Bartender's
Scam Bible
by
Peter Francis & R.Chip DeGlinkta

First Edition, 2005

Scam Bible®
The In the Know Series® and Scambible.com®
are registered trademarks of Promethean Books.

Library of Congress Control Number: 2003116399
ISBN: 0-9748677-0-5

Printed in the United States of America

Published by
Promethean Books
1000 Bourbon Street #250
New Orleans, Louisiana
70116
www.prometheanbooks.com

This book is available at quantity discounts for bulk purchases.
For more information, call 1-888-672-9018.

Art and Design by Nigel Pickhardt and Travis Klein

This is a work of fiction. All characters herein are imaginary.
Any resemblances to persons living or dead are completely coincidental.
The authors in no manner whatsoever endorse or encourage acts
of theft or the application of this material to existing situations.
The scenarios described herein are untested, completely fictitious,
and are intended as a parody of the restaurant industry, nothing more.

To Adolfo Rollo

Special thanks to Mr. Shing-a-Ling,
Mom, Smeller,
Travis Klein, John Scalo,
Family, Friends,
Venus, & Aphrodite.

Contents

~∾ *Foreword* ∾~

It is not common for the editor of a book to also write its foreword, as I am and I do here. It is in fact highly uncommon. Yet this is a highly uncommon work. It was completely by accident that I stumbled onto its authors, and indeed I was quite unprepared for the discovery. While taking lunch at a Bourbon Street restaurant (which shall now and forever go nameless), I was importuned to overhear an extraordinarily colorful and wildly ostentatious conversation between the two on-duty waiters. From my earnest vantage point I was delighted to surreptitiously drink-in this new voice I was hearing in snippets and stops, and intended to borrow it for some project or other in the future. My table, serendipitously crammed next to their work station, allowed me a perfect juxtapose for this odd and quixotic recital. The talk centered mostly on the exploits and adventures of a mysterious character referred to as "Pump" or the "Handle", and the hilariously nefarious things this Pump would do or say. Of course the more I heard the more I suspected that the waiters had discovered their audience and were having a laugh at my expense, so unbelievable and exaggerated were their reminisces.

When at last, without thinking, I let out an uncontrollable guffaw at one of the more ribald anecdotes, I realized that the waiters had in fact been entirely unaware of my existence, because no sooner had the trembling laughter escaped my guilty abdomen than they looked at each other aghast, realizing

11

for the first time that they were being listened to, and not another word was exchanged between them. A check was produced and I was soon on my way.

Over the ensuing week or two I often found myself revisiting that overheard conversation and tried to dismiss it and its contents from my mind. But I could not. Feeling a jolt of initiative I decided instead to heed my editorial instinct and pursue the story.

Nothing could have prepared me for what was to happen next. I found myself back at the restaurant and this time I forthrightly queried the two waiters. Were the stories I eavesdropped on true? Did this Pump character really exist? Who is this person known as the Handle? Could I meet them?? What other juicy stories were left untold??? I clearly intimated that we (Promethean Books) were willing to pay handsomely for the information.

In time and with a marked reluctance on their behalf I was able to persuade these odd yet likable characters to reveal the whole story and to my utter amazement I was ushered into a world of insight and knowledge that I truly had no previous concept of. It was as though these street-toughened working boys had smote me with the divine blade of enlightenment, and I was grateful and deeply honored to be smote.

While I was in the office one early morning working on a text with the usual deadlines hovering closely overhead, having all but given up on the stubborn waiters' willingness to collaborate, I looked up from my desk and was startled to see Chip and Peter standing before me. In their possession was a tattered handful of dog-eared notebooks. I was loath to read their prose and poetry, as I suspected that they were intending me to deliver on their lifelong ambitions to be writers and poets, and for a day perhaps, not waiters and bartenders. I shuddered to think that I would be obliged to give their efforts at the very least a cursory edit and a few encouraging tips. I was stunned when instead they presented me with what they referred to as the "Bible". In their hands they held an underground manuscript, passed from knowing hand to knowing hand, barman to barman, waiter to waiter, and in this jumbled almanac lay the skeleton and rudiments of what is now known as *The Infamous Waiter & Bartender's Scam Bible*. I realized instantly the importance of the work before me, but was the last of the triumvirate to suspect its real potential. Peter and Chip were leagues ahead of me. They suppositioned that I become their editor and that they intended to right this flotsam and jetsam into a cohesive and coherent "How To" manual. That was over two years ago at this writing, and after much hard work and diligent editing the opus took shape.

Before you now is the most original, unique, and authentic artifact of its kind or any kind and I hope you enjoy it. I did.

Ched M. Mardo

Assistant Editor, Promethean Books.
New Orleans. 2004.

Introduction

 **Gas and Matches**

"Nothing is true, everything is permitted."
-William S. Burroughs

You are dining at your favorite restaurant. The food is toothsome and divine, the service crisp and attentive; even the amiable and glowing manager has come to the table to offer a warm toast. You leave a ridiculously lavish gratuity and sashay out the front door with an air of boozy self-importance. On the way out, you get hep with the busboy and jive with the porter, who both quietly indulge you as the eager manager maudlinly whisks you into a waiting cab, and off you go. What a night! You feel like you are really something special….and you are, but to none more special than to the attentive waiter, who just hosed you down like a champ and played your sorry ass like a finely tuned violin.

Don't feel bad. You weren't the first, and you certainly won't be the last, and besides, you weren't necessarily duped by some easily-detectable scam either. Chances are it was executed quite nimbly, with all the subtle dexterity of a well-practiced illusion, albeit one in which you were an unwilling and oblivious participant.

Until now, only our hero, the perpetrating waiter, and a few discreet co-conspirators were able to truly appreciate the enormously entertaining and satisfying enterprise of systematically ripping off a restaurant and its customers. After years of working on the notorious *Bourbon Street* of New Orleans, legendary as the fountainhead and forum of every conceivable restaurant and bar scam known to mankind, two straight-shooting waiters, at the top of their game, share their combined experience of what has largely existed as an indistinct oral history (occasionally misrepresented by square-headed outsiders pretending to be in the know). Here at last, in all its unabashed glory, in print, and organized in a way that encourages careful study but retains the lighthearted humor of this ingenious and underappreciated craft, is the cult classic, the underground "how to" smash hit, the absolute and indispensable insider's authority on service-industry hijinks bar none: *The Infamous Waiter & Bartender's Scam Bible.*

The scenarios that follow all share the same short list of characters: the Customer, the Manager, and the Waiter*. Allow us to introduce you.

The Customer- Often kind and unselfish, at times cruel and even parsimonious; we need not speak too poorly of our esteemed benefactor (although it is difficult to speak too highly of him either), without whom none of this would be possible. At one time or another we have all eaten out, and in doing so, taken a stab at this leading role. Let's give ourselves a big round of applause!

The Manager- "FloorDick", "The Mope", "Schmoo", etc., the restaurant manager has acquired many apt nicknames over

---

*The waiter and bartender are treated as identical for the purposes of this book as their duties overlap and are even combined in certain fortuitous situations where a waiter is allowed to prepare his own alcoholic drinks, or a bartender is forced to serve food like a common waiter. More often than not, the term "waiter" will be used to refer to both. Considerations particular to the bar are covered in detail in Chapter 12.

the years depending on his or her particular demeanor or physical appearance. Overworked, undersexed, ill-endowed, and roundly scorned by all, perhaps the only creature more ridiculous is the one who actually gets collared by this bleary-eyed invertebrate. But watch out! Anything is possible, and nothing is more nauseating than to witness a momentarily actualized manager rooting out and beheading the goose that lays the golden eggs.

Customers and waiters alike are always looking to have a few laughs at the manager's expense. It isn't out of the ordinary for FloorDick to stand emasculated as a pugnacious customer berates him in the most humiliating fashion, or for a waiter, with a mind for some cheap entertainment, to somehow get a hold of his keys and throw them in the trash, sending the old boy chasing after his own tail for a spell!

The Waiter- It is a myth that all waiters are dormant intellectuals or artists. In truth, some are even dumber than the managers. But who wants to read about them? The *Scam Bible* concerns itself almost exclusively with the *modus operandi* of one very specific and elusive breed of waiter. Known in certain tight-lipped and educated circles as the Employee of the Month, for commonly masquerading as the most dependable and hardworking of waiters, he is more aptly referred to as simply, the Pump Handle, for his uncanny ability to quickly and quietly erect an ever-pumping money siphon of scam wherever he goes, capable of yielding literally truckloads of tax-free banknotes.

As the only conscious player in the game, the waiter shuffles the unwitting manager and guest around and against each other in a whirring blur of Two-Card Monty. The manager is sent to investigate a fictitious customer complaint... a trayload of free drinks is passed illicitly over the bar. The "Pump Handle" deals out a little strategic sympathy to "the Mope"... she is momentarily distracted as his partner in crime slips a case of dungeouness crabs and some top-shelf booze out the rear entrance. Luau!

Hijacking armloads of seafood and liquor will make you the life of the party, but it won't pay your light bill. To generate actual cash money, three things must occur.

1. The inventory must be delivered to the customer in the form of food and drink ordered from a menu.

2. The waiter must manipulate a variety of important elements in such a way as to undetectably intercept all or a worthwhile portion of the payment rendered.

3. The payment must be rendered in cash.**

The problem is that any customer with more than a mouthful of brains expects to receive an itemized bill of sale or "check" prior to payment, and the restaurant not only expects to retain a receipt of the final transaction, but requires the waiter to submit intermittent tickets along the way as he obtains items from different departments that are out of his jurisdiction, such as the bar or the kitchen. In other words, the waiter cannot simply yell out an order for a couple of steaks to the cooks, help himself to a few martinis from the bar, and scrawl an arbitrary total on a napkin in lieu of an actual check.

The genius of the sticky-fingered waiter lies is in his ability to provide the restaurant and customer with the necessary documentation, and at the same time maintain a steady, sucking vortex of company dollars. Many years of working with this objective in mind have yielded a standard repertoire of principles and technique, a portfolio of smoke and mirrors utilized instinctively by Pump Handles the world over to exploit the cracks in a restaurant's system.

It should be noted that the systems by which a restaurant regulates its sales and safeguards its profits vary greatly from one operation to the next. Some use no more than a prim-

---

**An exception to this rule is when a "Carrion Check" is available, described in Chapter 20.*

18

itive system of hand-written checks, while others use high-tech computer terminals to coordinate every aspect of restaurant activity. The *Scam Bible* embraces the entire spectrum of this technology. It takes the reader on a comprehensive journey from the classics to the cutting edge.

It is only by witnessing firsthand the work of a few amazingly talented and legendary Pump Handles that this book could be written, although we were obliged, by their sheer ballsiness, to include a number of the daring exploits of reckless but creative *up and comers* as well. The writers have made every attempt to put the readers in the driver's seat as often as possible, as though they were executing the scams themselves. Important concepts have been set out in italics and a comprehensive glossary of technical terms has been added at the rear of the book, so that the layman will not be left outside the loop. Our hope in sharing this privileged viewpoint, is not only that the dining experience of the casual reader be infused with a little more adventure and intrigue, but most importantly that the hard-working waiter will give himself a well-deserved raise.

Without further adieu, we are proud to present you with enough high-octane gasoline to reduce any "House" to a pile of crackling cinders. So what the hell are you waiting for? Got a match?

Peter Francis and R. Chip DeGlinkta

How to BURN DOWN the HOUSE

1

⇜ *The Buffet Scam* ⇝

*"Facing a Zen Master on the road,
meet him neither with words nor silence.
Give him an uppercut, and you will be called
one who understands Zen."*
-Ekai (1183-1260)

The Scam: The original recycled check move is much beloved for its speed and simplicity...and for the fat stacks of cash bucks it generates!

This one is as old and elusive as Truth itself, and strikes with the same profound and quizzical ease. But you don't need to be the Dali Lama to profit from this ancient wisdom. Continually presenting a single check to multiple tables for payment and repayment is a hallmark of an entry-level scamster with an eye for advancement.

Like so:

1. During a breakfast, lunch, or dinner buffet a table orders two buffets and two iced teas. They eat, pay cash, and leave.

2. Save the ticket.

3. You get another table. They order the same thing:
    two buffets and two iced teas.

4. You serve them the same ticket as the previous table;
    they pay and leave.

5. You are left with the one ticket and twice the total, plus tips.

6. Skim the excess and get back to work!

Unfortunately, everyone in your section is not always eating and drinking the exact same thing, but if you know how to improvise, you can weave those rough edges into fine green lace. Remember...

Don't Be Afraid to Put the Square Block in the Round Hole! Let's say you have a ticket from a previous customer for two buffets and two sodas. You want to use it again on a current table, but they are drinking two iced teas. Serve the check anyway! If they ask, tell them you rang in two sodas instead of two iced teas by mistake, but not to worry, because they are the same price. Who cares if they think you're stupid? You got paid!

Cash In On that Short-Term Memory Loss! People love to get away with things and you can use this to your advantage. For example, there are two tables in your section, two people at each table, and each person is eating the buffet. The problem is that one table is drinking iced tea and the other is drinking beer. Forget to ring in the teas, so that you can use the ticket on the beer table as well.

1. Ring in only two buffets, print out the ticket, and save it.

2. Pull up the ticket again and ring in the two beers, so that
    you can get them from the bar. Print that ticket and save it.

3. You now have two copies of the same ticket at different stages- one with two buffets, and one with two buffets and two beers.

4. When it's time to pay up, serve the earlier copy of the ticket, the one without any drinks on it, to the table that had iced tea. They will think- "Wow, that jerk waiter forgot to ring up our iced teas! We saved three bucks!" They will pay quickly and slink out, thinking they got away with something.

5. Serve the beer-drinking table the latter copy of the ticket, with the beers on it. There is nothing amiss here, so they'll pay and leave.

6. Finally, although you only rang in two buffets and two beers, you have the cash for four buffets and two beers.

7. Take your cut and give the restaurant theirs. Fair is fair, right?

"Forgetting" to charge for something is a good way to hurry-up any unfriendly table during a scam. They will think they really stuck it to you, and will want to quickly settle up and leave before you catch your "mistake".

The Bohemian: There is one in every crowd. His friend is having the buffet, but he just wants a burger and fries, which of course has to come from the kitchen. No worries. The Wagon Wheel (see Chapter 20) is handy here. Spin a new check off a buffet on a previous check and ring in your burger and fries. Touchdown!

There are many possible obstacles and solutions. We assume that if you had the brains to buy a copy of the *Scam Bible,* you must have some real creative flair- so use it!

25

Playing It Off: This one usually happens just a little too fast for the average FloorDick, but if you find one that can blink and count at the same time: proceed with caution. You are easily caught if someone is keeping an eye on your checks or tables. If you do get pinched, feigning confusion and invoking the old Honest Mistake is probably your best bet. The important thing is to never fess up. You might be eligible for unemployment!

2

✒ *The Bastards* ✒

*"All who could flee went to hide in the mountains,
climbing the steepest rocks to escape these abominable,
merciless, predator-like people."*
-Bartolomé de la Casas

The Scam: Nothing can be more vexing or discouraging to
the hard working and under appreciated waiter than to fall vic-
tim to the dreaded Walk-Out. The bastards skip out on the tab,
leaving the waiter in the lurch, while determinedly eroding his
cash intake. On the other hand, nothing can be more pleasing
and rewarding than to serve up a convincing dose of Phony
Walk-Out, especially if there is a bleeding heart FloorDick on
the staff. Here is what we mean.

1. Pick your moment with extreme shrewdness, there is no
   room for error with this particular approach.

2. Be certain that the manager is busy, in fact, the busier the
   better. More importantly make sure he is the sympathetic
   and trusting sort, a Good Samaritan, and perhaps even new
   on the job.

3. Single out a table that has the tell-tale look of a Dine and Dasher: dead heads, hillbillies, punk rockers, and other shifty oddball types.

4. Present the check quickly, collect even more quickly, and of course, cash only! Move far away from the table to perform some other essential task. Tend to another section, discuss an imagined problem with the manager or assist a fellow waiter in need. In any case, be sure the table in question has vacated the premises and is well out of the picture.

5. Hurriedly discover the walk-out and dash outside in a feigned attempt at giving chase. Agitatedly query your fellow workers if they "collected on table 12!!??" or did they "see which way they went!!??". Frantically search the restrooms and other dining areas for the interlopers, finally resigning yourself to the obvious fact that you've been unfairly victimized by walk-out guests. Appear to be boiling mad at the unfairness of it all, bite your thumbs and pull your hair for theatrical effect. All the while spitting sworn oaths of venomous revenge should you ever cross their tracks again and so on.

6. Inform the manager of the terrible turn of events, exasperatingly relating the details and portraying yourself as momentarily distracted while selflessly helping an overwhelmed fellow waiter to get caught up.

7. Let the Good Samaritan take pity on you and void the check. Assure him that you will never allow anyone to take advantage of you like that again, and thank him warmly for understanding. Now pull yourself together and get back to work!

We have seen this scam reap some mighty windfalls when applied properly. And it always makes FloorDick come away feeling like a real friend to the working stiff.

Playing It Off: Should the Good Samaritan suddenly go bad and become suspicious or uncooperative, just relax and stay cool. He may only comp half or a portion of the bill to teach you a lesson, but why should you care? You already collected the whole total, plus tip. Grumble under your breath about how unfair life is.

3

～ Suggestive Stealing ～

"The enlightened waiter makes his own luck."
-R. Chip DeGlinkta

The Scam: Only a dope waits around for the perfect opportunity to drop out of the clear blue sky. By helping the customer make decisions that facilitate fruitful scamming, the intelligent waiter precipitates his own good fortune.

Create the Necessary Opportunities to Work Your Favorite Angles.

1. Convince successive guests to order the same items, thereby increasing your chances to re-use checks.

2. Convince guests to order items that you can get your hands on without a ticket and make more money in the self-service industry (see Chapter 9).

3. Convince a guest to order a particular item that you need to complete a profitable maneuver, i.e.- if you have a ripe old ticket for two lunch buffets, do not push the swiss and bacon burger.

Cheat If You Have To. If push comes to shove and no one is responding to your suggestions, 86 competitive items until you get the order that you need: "I'm sorry, M'am. We just ran out of vodka. Might I suggest a local draft beer instead?"

Blend In. Maintain a low profile by suggesting inventory that is difficult to track. If you are skimming the bar, draft beers are less traceable than bottles. If it's coming from the kitchen, move inconspicuous entrees that can be quickly and easily prepared, rather than steaks or complicated items that take a while to cook.

Playing It Off: If you're not careful, you might make Employee of the Month. Suggestive selling is too much work for most waiters, so your manager is going to be delighted to see you taking the initiative.

4

~ *Houston...We Have a Problem.* ~

"Open the pod bay door, Hal."
-Dave, 2001: A Space Odyssey

The Scam: "Jeez, I'm in the f⬛🐷🐸 weeds!" the waiter thinks to himself one busy Saturday night. "O.k., table 12 needs 3 margaritas, 1 no salt, 2 light beers and a vodka martini straight up with a twist and an olive. I need to get a drink order from 18, bread for 21 and uh...What the hell's that fat ass givin' me the eye for? Oh yeah, I forgot his damn sour cream. Keep your pants on, Porky. I'm comin'... Let's see what table 14 left me...Crap! 2 on 50!? What's wrong with these cheapskates anyway? There must be a convention of pawn shop owners in town. I really needed to make some cash tonight, but at this rate I'll be lucky to walk outta here with 20 bucks!...What's that?! No shit, FloorDick! I know my food's dyin' in the window, you f😡🐷🔪🪓 eunuch!! If only NumbNuts here would get off the damn computer I could put this order in and pick it up!"

Our hero tries to punch in his order when suddenly, "Squawk! Crackle! System error! System error!...Blip."

The screen goes blank.

"Hmm..." says the waiter softly, "maybe things aren't so bad after all."

Houston...?

The computer goes down and confusion reigns. You are floating once again in that old familiar vacuum, free from all the tedious obstructions of modern technology. When the electronics go on the fritz, the management will switch to a system of handwritten checks. Generally, these checks are made up of two carbon copies attached to a hard copy. The carbon copies are for the customer and the kitchen, and the hard copy is for the records. There are two basic models for this category of restaurant tomfoolery.

File 13: To the artless novice, the Crumpled-up Check may represent the only scam he has brains enough to pull off, but that does not detract from its unrivaled potential for earning. Over the years, its ridiculous dividends have sung their siren song to many a deft and talented veteran as well. It does not get much simpler, or better, than this.

1. A customer orders, eats, and pays.

2. The Waiter trashes the check and pockets the entire cash payment, as if the transaction never existed.

Destroy all the evidence! Get in the habit of taking your carbon copy from the kitchen whenever possible.

Unfortunately, you will most likely be issued a sequential stack of checks and asked to account for each one at the end of your shift. If too many come up missing, you will inevitably get the axe. The trick here is to tap into another source of tickets for use with your cash-paying tables, so that your check sequence is unaffected. The Pump Handle still has a few tickets stashed from the last system failure, while the rest of us might have to steal a stack from FloorDick or a fellow waiter.

The Carbon Copy Differential: If you are unable to get your hands on any extra checks, not to worry; a lot can happen between the customer's carbon copy and the hard copy that must be turned in at the end of your shift. This method requires a little more finesse, but is impervious to the Sequential Ticket Defense, and is much safer overall.

1. The customer orders a steak, 2 lbs of crawfish, a salad, and an iced tea.

2. Write down only what you cannot get without a ticket, in this case, the steak.

3. Turn in the kitchen's copy to get your steak, and rustle up the rest of the items yourself.

4. When it comes time to pay, place a piece of cardboard between the customer's carbon copy and the hard copy and carefully tally out the bill on the *customer's copy.* Include all the items with the correct tax, and collect the full amount in cash.

5. You are left with the hard copy that only indicates the steak. Total this out with the correct tax, and this is the ticket that you will turn in at the end of the shift. *Be sure you do not write directly on the hard copy!* Place an old carbon copy on top as you total it out, to make it look natural.

In the end you are left with the tidy differential of the two copies.

Playing It off: Buy your manager a drink at the pub afterwards and openly marvel at his managerial acumen. Just be sure he gets a barstool with a nice soft cushion.

5

ᘏᕒ *Putting Them on Ice* ᘏᕒ

"Lights, cameras, action!"

The Scam: A faulty credit card machine is a handy item to carry in your bag of tricks! This method incorporates a bit of playacting as you pretend that the credit card terminal is inoperable or the card itself is unusable. In this way, the waiter attempts to inconvenience the customer into switching to a cash transaction. For Example:

You are looking to split a check with a crooked manager (see Chapter 15) and the customer unwittingly stymies the operation by pulling out a credit card.

Waiter *(in a helpful tone)*- "Just to let you know, Sir. The credit card terminal has been sort of temperamental today. This may take a while. Would cash be more convenient for you?"

If the customer pressures you to run it anyway, disappear with his card for 5 or 10 minutes, then pop back in to let him know you're still trying, but really to see if he's ready to dummy up. No? Turn'em and burn'em. Run the card and move on to the next customer.

Or, if the customer is already at the counter...

Take his card, swipe it incorrectly a few times and pretend to try to make it work, but to no avail.

Waiter *(with a good sense of humor, looking up from time to time to see if the customer is ready to play ball)* - "Jeez! This thing is always on the blink!" or "Sorry Sir, I'm afraid this happens all the time. Sometimes it takes a while." etc.

Once again- don't fight it too hard. No green? No problem. Next!

Turning a couple of would-be credit card transactions to cash at the last minute is good for appearances. Use it to normalize your checkout as you are winding down after an overzealous day of scamming and there are not enough cash transactions to make everything look legit.

Playing It Off: This is one scam that the poor manager really has a hard time catching, much less substantiating, but suppose he walks right up while the customer is waiting and catches your performance in mid-scene...

Waiter *(without missing a beat)* - "Oh, hey Joe. Can you try running this card for me? I'm having a hard time with it."

The manager runs the card, it magically goes thru, he feels special, you walk away clean, and the customer is none the wiser.

6

～ *El Cannibal* ～

"E tu, Brutus?"
- Julius Caesar

The Scam: No friends? No wonder. But at least you can buy some more crack. Picking up credit card payments from your fellow waiters without picking up the corresponding sales, is a cold-hearted scam this waiter learned the hard way. Here's how to cannibalize your coworkers.

1. Steal a neighbor's signed credit card slip (one without a memorable tip).

2. Go to a credit card terminal, pull it up, and enter the tip.

3. Go to the *change server number* function.

4. Change the existing server number to your server number.

5. Throw away the original signed copy.

6. When you turn in your credit card report, the payment will have magically appeared on your list of transactions. Tell the manager that you lost the signed copy. He'll let it ride, the customer won't contest it, and you'll wind up in the green.

The unlucky waiter must still compensate the house for the sale, but has been anonymously relieved of the means to do so. Congratulations and wipe your chin off. Does it really taste like pork?

Playing It Off: It's hard to pick up on this backstab, especially if it was a busy shift, but if you do get caught, run don't walk. Our advice? Get a life you parasite!

7

⁓ *Leftovers* ⁓

"One man gathers what another man spills."
- Robert Hunter

The Scam: This approach not only pays a handsome stipend when properly executed but is just plain fun to pull off. Using a hardly eaten entree as a prop, the waiter seeks to cash in on a dissatisfied guest that never existed. If you have a greenhorn in the ranks of your management team this can be a good way to exploit their inexperience and add some heft to your wallet. It works effectively on seasoned vets as well, but be wary: even a restaurant manager can have a moment of fleeting clarity, especially if you try to go to the bank on this too often.

Here's how it goes.

1. A diner barely touches his entree. Clear the table as usual but set the untouched entree aside.

2. Present and settle the check.

3. Approach the Mope and, full of aloof concern, explain that the customer did not touch his or her entree and casually inquire if it could be voided from the check. Present her with the plate of cold and untouched food as evidence.

4. Be certain not to intimate that there is a pressing complaint. We don't want her to approach the table and start poking her nose into our little subterfuge.

5. After she voids the entree from the check, pocket the cash and be sure to thank her.

Only attempt this gentle ruse when the House is busy and your manager is all alone, insuring that a table-side inquiry into the matter is very unlikely.

Playing It Off: This one is tough to pick up on, but if the Mope does happen to approach the table, just play it cool. The customer will view it as competent management concerned with a sub-par product. You are in the clear either way and undoubtedly have gained the quiet admiration of your managerial staff for your dedication to service and attention to detail.

8

Evil Incorporated

"We can't all be saints."
-John Dillinger

The Scam: The gang bang. A little honor amongst thieves goes a long way. Teaming up with a tight-lipped buddy opens limitless windows of opportunity and makes the game a lot more enjoyable. You are calculating, organized, and well-rehearsed, and now you have someone to share it all with. There is only one corporate by-law: all cash intake is split fifty-fifty at the end of each shift, regardless of who collects more. Anything is possible now, but here's a few ideas to get you started.

Walking the dog: Take your FloorDick out of the picture for a bit, while your partner hoses the place down. Engaging him with banal questions usually does the trick, but drop a trayload of food if you have to.

Trading tickets: There is no reason to miss out on anything. Between the two of you, there are tickets for every combination. I can see it now...

"Hey man, you got a ticket for two buffets and two teas?"

"Let's see... yup! Say, you don't have anything open with a couple of dozen oysters, do you?"

"Yes, Sir. They just left."

"Great! Listen, you pick up table 14 in my section. They just want two beers and two dozen oysters, and you can Wagonwheel using that old check."

"Sounds like a plan. Hey, where's the Mope anyway?

"Oh, she's all hung over, as usual. I think she's in the office cryin' in her coffee (guffaw, guffaw)."

"Oh well...did you bring the one hitter?"

Clean-up: With an extra man, covering your tracks is a cinch. If your cash sales are suspiciously low, your partner can "buy" a credit card slip (see Chapter 17) or let you pick up a table that is obviously going to pay cash, to even things out. Also, rehearse explanations and alibis for every possible scenario so that you can help each other wriggle out of awkward situations.

Agree on a few code words or phrases for warnings and quick communication, for example: "Anchovie!" = The manager is coming.

Playing It off: It's a much safer game with two players, but if you do get caught: partnership dissolved.

9

≫ *Su Casa, Mi Casa* ≪

"Property is theft."
-Leon Trotsky

The Scam: Depending on how much inventory is readily available, and how obtuse your manager is, opening your own restaurant within a restaurant could be a shrewd business move. Without ever approaching a register, the working man's waiter can rustle-up an ample feast. For example: a dozen oysters to start off, an iced tea, the soup and salad combo, and for desert, the key lime pie with a cup a'joe to wash it all down. Yum, yum...sounds like a tasty hit!

Food and drink that you can get your hands on without ringing in a corresponding ticket is just like a wellspring of free money. One legendary scam master even sold the menus! There are many ways to work the self-service angle. Here's two or three.

With a Recycled Check Maneuver (see chapter 1):

1. You have a previous ticket for two burgers, two salads, and two iced teas.

2. Another table orders the exact same thing: two burgers, two salads, and two iced teas.

3. You *only* ring in what you cannot get yourself: the two burgers.

4. You fetch your customers the self-serve items, *without ringing them in*.

5. When it's time to drop the check, you drop the previous ticket and collect for all the items, leaving you with the excess cash for two iced teas and two salads.

Congrats amigo! You just gave yourself a raise!

With the Wagonwheel (see chapter 20): Spin off the self-service food items as well as the drinks. Spreading it around like this will help to keep liquor costs from looking suspicious, without slowing down your business.

Verbal Totals: Walk right up and tell them the total, or use your register as a prop, hitting a few buttons and making it beep for effect. Be sure you figure in the correct tax so that everything will match up, in case you have to ring it in at the last minute.

Handwritten checks: Write it all out nice and neat, and serve it just like any other check. These work just fine, but if you get caught, they are evidence against you.

Playing It Off: If they nab you serving a handwritten check, there isn't too much space to wiggle out of it. Even a restaurant manager can put that together. But, here's one way to plan for the worst:

1. Make sure the total on the fake check is correct and includes the local tax rate.

2. Just before serving the fake check, punch in the entire order on the computer but do not total it out. Just leave it on the screen.

3. If you feel the heat closing in (either the manager is talking with the table or is hovering dangerously close), *total the order on the screen, and then very quickly close it out completely.*

4. When the manager approaches with the fake check and questions you, simply tell him that you had no other choice but to write it out by hand, because you accidentally closed it out on the machine and could not print a copy to give to the customer.

5. He'll then check your closed checks, find it and apologize. Then you can play it up a little- "Oh, No problem, man! I understand. I know it looked a little suspicious, but blah blah blah..." Blow a little smoke up his ass just for appearances, and then turn the hose back on.

This is a great one to team up on. You serve the fake check, while your buddy keeps his eye on the manager and rings it up under your server number if need be.

10

⚜ *Friendly Delivery* ⚜

**"When the strike of a hawk breaks the body of its prey,
it is because of timing."**
-Sun Tzu

The Scam: Wholesale transferral of stock from the restaurant's shelves to yours is a high risk/high reward endeavor and not for the faint of heart. Getting cases of steaks, seafood, liquor, and other pricey inventory to disappear out the back door can be tricky. It also makes for high adventure. Orchestrate this little dance wisely and keep a close eye on the Mope. If she snaps out of it and catches you in the act, it might mean jail time. Achtung baby!

This scam has three stages.

1. **Selection and placement for pickup:** Select your quarry wisely. Steaks, lobster tails, cases of fine wine and top shelf spirits are all worthy candidates. Deposit the goods in a place where they can be swept into a passing trash can, dumpster, mop bucket, bus tub, clothes hamper, duffel bag, or other concealing receptacle of your choice. Go from stage 1 to stage 2 without delay and without attracting attention.

2. **Pick-up and placement for final delivery:** While the Mope is preoccupied with some time consuming crisis of your design, transfer the trash can, bus tub, etc., containing your valuables to the pick up point, perhaps the dumpster or a concealed, accessible area of the parking lot, for final delivery. Progress from stage 2 to stage 3 and make it look natural.

3. **Final delivery and departure:** Pick up your goodies from the designated spot as soon as possible. We advise incorporating a partner at this stage as you will not always be able to run it out to your car and may not want to involve a busboy or other employee. It is much cleaner to have a friend, who has nothing to do with the restaurant, swing by, throw the stuff into his car, and drive away than it is to leave the evidence in your car until you get off work. Prearrange the pick up spot and call him once you have everything in place. If you don't have any friends, park your car in close proximity to the House and generously tip a busboy or your dishwasher to toss the loot in your trunk, while you keep an eye on the Mope. Now get back to work and keep your eyes and ears open; there is money to be made here.

Hijacking stock from your restaurant is like going on an all expense paid shopping spree. Though primarily a technique employed by busboys and cooks, the Friendly Delivery approach can be utilized by any enterprising opportunist. We have had the pleasure of seeing this taken to the extreme on Bourbon Street by a virtual deity of scam. This legendary busboy delivered cases of frozen shrimp and steaks to nearby restaurants on a pre-order basis. He would bag the orders in the freezer and stuff them into a clean garbage can topped off with some harmless trash. When he made his trash dump rounds, he would scoot around the corner and drop off his orders as previously arranged, and we hear that he always gave a generous deal!

Playing It Off: Good luck if the Mope stumbles onto your gold-lined trash can. Your only chance is to offer her half of the steaks and promise to never let it happen again.

11

ᕯᕧ *The Jail Break* ᕧᕯ

**"*I am not a liberator, liberators do not exist,
the People liberate themselves.*"
-Ernesto "Che" Guevara

The Scam: We picked this up from a dirty busboy who had a soft spot for deadbeat guests. He was offering half off if they were willing to pay cash and slip out discreetly, *without* saying goodbye to their waiter. This is is how he made the pages of the *Scam Bible.*

1. He would keep his eyes peeled for what seemed to be open minded customers: goth types, frat boys hot for kicks, Texans, or stinking Frenchmen.

2. Once he had a gut feeling about someone, he would make a pass or two, prebussing a dish or refilling an iced tea, and test the waters with a few harmless overtures.

3. Only when he was sure of their corruptibility would he dive into the incriminating proposition.

4. For half the check or so in cash up front, he would signal the customers when their waiter was sufficiently distracted and the coast was clear for them to sneak out of the restaurant without paying the bill.

5. If they accepted, he would take the cash, drop back, and watch for the proper moment.

6. The moment would come, he would signal the guests, and they would make for the door.

7. The busser would keep on bussing and the waiter would be left scratching his head.

Busboys with this kind of weaponry have real potential.

Playing It Off: The details of this operation became clear only after the busboy's assistance fell short and the escapees were run down by their angry waiter, which points to a possible drawback: the sort of people that are daring enough to play along with this scam are the ones that an experienced waiter is likely to keep a close eye on. The ambitious busperson did the right thing however, and denied everything.

12

~ *Private Reserve* ~

"Yo Ho Ho and a Bottle o' Rum..."
-Sailor's Folk Song

The Scam: Bartenders, like blondes, have all the fun. Behind the bar, your only limitation is your guilty conscience, but constant scamming and poor technique will quickly drive the House liquor costs through the roof and attract the attention of the resident PricknBalls. Implementing and adhering to a few tried and true rules of the trade will keep your operation running smoothly, all the while insuring that the company man won't be poking his snout into your money trough.

1. Run a tight ship. You are on display so play the part. Convey a no-nonsense sensibility about yourself to guests, co-workers, and management.

2. Approach the bar like a card dealer approaches a blackjack table. Read each and every player and deal to them accordingly. If he's toasted, jack up the price; if she's old and senile, give her half a shot; if they are big time tippers, give them one on the House.

3. Short pour every chance you get, especially in drinks that call for juices and sweet mixers. Shorting frozen drinks is a cinch as well, just pour a little rotgut into the straw for that whopping first sip.

4. Always short pour and downshelf drinks that are being prepared for any guests who are not right there at the bar, via cocktail waitresses or waiters with out of view sections.

5. Charge the highest prices possible with your legit guests and generate as many sales as you can. If one person is running a loose tab for a group be sure to add a goodly portion of phantom drinks to it, top shelf and make it a double.

6. Occasionally stock the shelves yourself, and stiffen up a drink or two with your own "Private Reserve", namely a bottle or two of the cheap stuff, procured at your neighborhood liquor store before your shift. Either cap off some hot selling top shelf bottles with the generic brand equivalent, or bring in some self-purchased well liquor brands to donate to the cause, or both!

7. Depending on the situation, pocket your money as you go or keep a running tally in your head and take it from the drawer later.

The techniques mentioned here are specific to the bar. In addition, every other technique described in this book can be applied behind the bar as well, and generally with much less managerial scrutiny.

Playing It Off: Offset the impact of your incessant pilfering by generating sales and supplementing the scam depleted stock with cheaply bought liquors. In this way you can maintain your cost control requirements while continuing to mint money hand over fist. Give a little back and keep the big picture in focus, but most of all, keep the omnipresent PricknBalls in the dark.

13

☙ *The Pawn Game* ☙

"Excellence at chess is one mark of a scheming mind."
- Sherlock Holmes

The Scam:
Waiter vs. FloorDick, checkmate in three, Waiter to move.

Problem: The underpaid Waiter is badly in need of a fresh sack o'stinky and as usual, FD is playing his hardest to keep him from capturing the necessary Benjamins.

Round 1:
The Waiter has his hostess seat him two customers that fit the cash-paying profile. On his recommendation, they order two mint juleps and two dozen raw oysters.

FD lets go a doleful sigh, furrows his brow, and decides to comb the House for a sympathetic ear.

"Interesting...This could go either way."

Round 2:
The Waiter has his bartender make the drinks and his oyster shucker shuck the oysters in good faith, as per the usual agree-

ment. The customers enjoy everything and are ready to pay. The Waiter carefully hand writes a fake ticket with the correct tax and total and serves it. Check.

FD stops abruptly at the oyster bar, momentarily entranced by the nimble swish of the oyster shucker's knife. Something is surely amiss, but what? He cradles his chin pensively between his thumb and forefinger and shifts his gaze to the floor beneath his feet. Suddenly it hits him. Gasp! Without warning, he lurches downward, grabs the cuffs of his trousers and pulls them up past his ankles, his knees bowed outwards in a comical fashion. It's his socks! His socks are two completely different colors! Not again! Still doubled over and angrily clutching the tips of his pant legs, beet red and bug-eyed with horror and betrayal, he glares up at the Waiter like some ridiculous giant crab. He misses his mother and wishes he had a glass of her special warm buttermilk.

"Oh for goodness' sake FD! Keep your head in the game! There's mischief afoot!"

Round 3:
The Waiter collects the cash payment, destroys the fake check, and pockets the dollars and cents- Checkmate!

"No hard feelings FloorDick! Play again? This time try to concentrate."

As you can see the Waiter could not have pulled this off without the careful use of his pawns, in this case: the Hostess, the Bartender, and the Oyster Shucker.

Here is a list of the usual pawns with some tips on how they can help you tighten up your game.

The Hostess: She can be of great use to you by qualifying the customers as cash-paying or non cash-paying. Make her privy to the lucrative profile, e.g.- hill folk, certain ethnic groups, scrubby looking college kids, etc. Also, if you are generous with the hostess you will tend to get more tables.

The Busboy/Food Runner: One of the most versatile pieces on the board, the busboy moves freely throughout the restaurant helping out wherever you need him: keeping tabs on the manager and running distractions, communicating with your boys in the kitchen, minding your section while you do your business, and so on. If he is your food runner as well, then all the better. You can send him for self-serve items or to pick up free entrees from your cook without it looking suspicious.

The Waiter: Of course, if you are an exclusive member of Evil Incorporated (see Chapter 8) there are numerous way to utilize your compatriot, but even a regular old waiter is handy from time to time. If he is a pushover, send him to unwittingly occupy your manager with a silly question while you put the moves on a customer, or snag a couple of his entrees from the pick-up window and throw them in the trash while no one is looking. This will incite a flare-up between him and the line cooks as to whether or not the order has been made and inevitably the manager will be called away from his other duties to resolve it.

The Scam-Savvy Cook: Getting entrees without submitting tickets is the objective here. Only use this resource when you are absolutely sure of a cash transaction; the cook will want to be paid either way. Incorporating kitchen staff can be risky, especially if your scam becomes common knowledge in the galley. Pre-arrange the cash split, so as to avoid any untimely negotiations and recruit someone who can discreetly fill the orders without garnering suspicion or attention.

The Bartender: Most of these lucky bastards are up to their elbows in the till already and will know exactly where you are coming from when you approach them with the classic money making proposition: a few drinks here and there, no questions asked, in exchange for a fat tip at the end of the shift.

The Dishwasher: This is your back door man, and very useful if you need to use his trash can to make a Friendly Delivery (see Chapter 10). He is way overworked and way underpaid, so a few dollars go a long way.

Don't become the low man on your own totem pole! It is easy to lose control of your pawns if you use them too often. If you are not careful, there may come a day when a table says- "Hi, We're friends with Joey the cook. He said for us to come in whenever we wanted and you would tighten us up with some free drinks and a couple of ribeyes." Uh oh! Who is running the show now? If you are balls to the wall networking, someone is bound to talk, or worse yet, take control of the board and reduce you to a pawn in your own game. Hit this angle seldom and with discretion; keep everyone on a need to know basis, and keep your reputation to a minimum. Tip well, but do not over tip or let your pieces know how much you are really making.

It is not necessary to be in outright cahoots with someone to gain their assistance. If you are friendly and tip people out from time to time, they will more often than not dummy up a useful service or item without extra compensation or knowledge of your operation.

Playing It Off: Floordick will spray all over himself if he stumbles upon this multi-faceted scheme. Keep quiet and try not to tumble with the rest of the dominoes.

14

～✲ *Oops! Wrong Check!* ✲～

**"He gives his harness bells a shake
to see if there is some mistake"
- Robert Frost**

The **Scam:** Everybody makes mistakes, most of all a harried waiter with his hands full. Full of money that is. When circumstance allows, the simplest of intentional oversights can prove quite profitable. Hoodwinking guests into paying slightly higher yet similar checks is a sure way to increase your slice of the money pie and cover your ass at the same time. Get this.

1. Look for ripe candidates. Some diners peruse their dinner checks with a scholarly zeal, while others either barely glance or not at all. You want the latter.

2. Produce a guest check that is closely similar to the actual check but is higher in total price. This might come from a coinciding table or from a vast library of old checks that you have saved for just this occasion.

To induce favorable circumstances suggestive sell similar items table after table (see chapter 3).

3. Present the higher check to the guest with the lower total. Finalize the transaction as quickly as possible. Standby to collect payment and render change swiftly, discarding the inflated yet eerily similar check at first opportunity.

 This approach can be attempted repeatedly as circumstance, design, and coincidence dictate. It can be a huge boon to the waiter with a solid sack of stones and provides an endless source of entertainment. To be sure, managers are not the only ones who make the same mistakes over and over again.

Playing It Off: This scam is difficult to get nabbed on. If the manager stumbles into the picture farting some accusation or other, or should the guest raise question; simply feign a double take, peruse the check yourself, produce the pre-prepared correct check from your ready pocket, and serve it as if nothing had happened. "Oops! Wrong check!"

15

◥◎ *Our Man in Amsterdam* ◎◤

***"One influential friend is worth more than
one hundred gold coins."***
-Sicilian proverb

*T*he Scam: For the lonely old scamster, it is always reassuring
to find a kindred spirit amongst the opposition. A double agent
on the managerial staff is a good thing to keep in your pocket,
especially if he is willing to void an occasional cash transaction
and split the winnings fifty-fifty. Here is how the typical inside
man operates.

1. You settle up a sizable cash check, but do not finalize the
   transaction on the computer.

2. You bring the check to the attention of your easygoing
   manager.

3. The manager discreetly voids the transaction, leaving you
   with the payment only.

4. You nonchalantly pass him half the cash.

5. The two of you agree on a reason why the ticket was voided, just in case another manager or higher-up has questions. For example, with marked disinterest, "Oh yeah, I remember those a-holes. They said they saw a rat or something and started to make a big stink, so Phil just voided the whole check to shut'em up."

Enjoy a little easy money for once!

This is an irrefutably delectable hit and a steady payer, and your manager should be congratulated for finally putting two and two together, but do not be a fool and let him in on the details of your entire operation. The inner circle is reserved for waiters only, and a very select few at that.

Caution: *Floordick is often way too eager once he has been turned out, and if he is a gambler, he may lose his composure altogether. Choke up on the reins or his greed and inexperience will surely get you both pinched.*

Unlike you, the dirty manager is a one-trick pony and his overworked scam is bound to raise a red flag once he has several waiters on the payroll. If he starts to make you nervous, *accidentally* closing out your cash checks before he has a chance to whack them or telling him that you have had nothing but credit card transactions may help to lower your curiously high void to sales ratio, and reduce you to only a minor player in the eyes of the police.

Playing It Off: If the Loose Cannon gets picked up, let them cry conspiracy until the cows come home. In truth, you have done absolutely nothing, as mere waiters do not have the ability to void checks. If you have more voids than the average Joe, it is only because you are "all thumbs" when it comes to that fancy computer. Leave your ex-manager farting in the mud. It is, afterall, his own fault for having no self control.

16

~❧ *Extra! Extra! Read All About It!* ~

"Is everything we see or seem but a dream within a dream?"
-Edgar Allan Poe

The Scam: When the House is dumb enough to advertise free coupon offers, consider it Manna falling from the heavens and straight into your bank account. If you are one of the lucky ones and your restaurant runs the kind of promotion that entails redemption of food or drink coupons then your ship has truly come in, and it has a golden hull. Typically these coupons are for free cups of soup, buy one get one free entrees, a free dessert with the purchase of dinner, and other incentives of this nature. In any case, it's all free money for you so long as you can get your enterprising fives onto a limitless supply of the same coupons, and match them up with items from previous transactions.

If you are not in a restaurant that employs this business enhancing technique, perhaps you should take your brown nosing, sycophantic self to the nearest FloorDick for a kiss-ass suggestion session, and put a feather in his cap that has the look of gold to it.

Of course, you do not want to actually deal with the damn things. What could constitute more of a pain in the ass than legions of penny-pinching diners intent on a half-priced dinner or a free cup of soup du jour. In fact, the less successful the campaign is in actuality, the better it is for you! Confused? If the coupons are a popular item, it will be more difficult to matriculate your own bogus ones into the mix. Every shift you want to cash in on two or three fraudulent coupons, so if you are inundated with legitimate ones, it will logically shrink your window of opportunity. Essentially, you want to be the main beneficiary of the coupon campaign.

All you need to get started is a pair of scissors and some big brass balls.

1. When the FloorDicks take out a coupon ad in a local publication, be certain to get a stack of these yourself.

2. Carefully clip as many coupons as you can, and keep a few handy during every shift.

3. When the time is right, after the customer has paid and left, take one of these valuable clippings and attach it to a check that has a corresponding item, as though the discount was applied previous to the payment.

4. Deduct the amount of the promotional items during your checkout, or have Floordick void it on the spot, depending on the local policy.

In this way you are left with the cash incentive intended for the customer, and at the same time titillate your manager's pleasure centers as he falsely perceives a good return on his promotional endeavors.

Don't limit yourself to coupons. Liberally apply gift certificates or any sort of promotional material that can be made to correspond with one or more items on a previously paid ticket, thus making the equivalent amount of cash available for spending.

Playing It Off: It is of course prerequisite to maintain absolute silence about your methods; the last thing you want is a glut of coupon hoarding co-workers honing in on your gold brick. This can be a temporary windfall or a long-term money farm, just keep clipping those coupons and keep congratulating Mongo on his good ideas.

17

✂ *The Potemkin Voucher* ✂

"An empty sack can't stand up."
-Haitian proverb

The Scam: Selling the same credit card slip to more than one waiter is indeed a desperate act, but if you don't feel like kicking tonight and don't care if you have a job tomorrow- take the money and run!

A Note to the Outsider: When a waiter winds up with mainly credit card transactions at the end of a shift and does not have enough cash to pay himself the tips he has earned, he often sells a credit card slip to another waiter, that is, he exchanges a valid, signed voucher for the equivalent amount in cash.

The scam version goes like this:

1. Before selling the original, go to the credit card terminal and print out an extra copy of the voucher.

2. Trade the original signed voucher to a fellow server for cash as usual.

3. Find another server who is willing and sell him the copy. If he asks, tell him the customer walked out with the original.

4. You now have twice the amount of the original transaction, in cash.

Pass the savings on to your dealer.

Playing It Off: It is not beyond your short-changed super to notice this glaring scam. If you are found out, play dumb and quickly boogie on down the line before the other waiters have you surrounded.

18

～ *The Package Deal* ～

> *"Easy does it, patience wins out over force."*
> *-Toussaint L'Ouverture*

The Scam:

"4:30 a.m.!" says the Alarm Clock.

"Grumble, grumble" replies the Breakfast Waiter. "It's too late to be last night and too damn early to be this morning!."

"Plop, plop, fizz, fizz...glug, glug, glug... Buuurp!... hmm... RRRRRRIP! Krsplash! tinkle, tinkle, tinkle..."

No time for a leisurely poop and a glance at the sports page. The tour buses are coming! Throw on that monkey suit and..

"Slam! shuffle, shuffle..."

Get to work!

Still unconscious after your third cup of coffee, you drop a half-pan of scrambled eggs into place on the breakfast buffet and that is when you hear it. Your ears perk up, your eyes widen and your blood runs cold. It is barely perceptible at first, like a faraway drummer practicing a jerky uneven roll on a tile floor, but to you, an A.M. waiter working a seasonal gig at a big hotel, the sound is all too familiar: the distant clatter of canes and walkers in great numbers closing in from the hotel lobby; multiple bus loads of retirees bent on seeing twelve cities in two days and getting their fair share of the free meals included in their tour package. The click-clack of their hardware mingles with the subtler death rattle of a hundred pill organizers as these gentle blue-haired sweeties pour over the dining room like an unyielding pack of Mongols.

Wanton destruction ensues, and in the end you are left with a lousy stack of meal vouchers worth a meager $1.25 in gratuity each, to be tallied, taxed and paid on your next check two weeks from now- Ouch!

If the management decides to say "f🔥💧☁️ you" and court the tour groups with cheap labor, "f🌀☠️〰️🔥 them!"

We heard of a case where some patient waiters were able to do just that. Here's how.

The Right Way: At the end of each shift, the waiters were supposed to count all the meal vouchers that they had collected; go to the computer; access the "voucher screen", and enter the correct monetary value of all their vouchers combined, e.g.- 10 vouchers @ $1.25 each = $12.50. This in turn went through the system and showed up on their next paycheck.

The Smart Way: The angry waiters' approach was identical, except for one thing. Rather than entering the correct monetary total, they would alter it ever so slightly, for instance $112.50 instead of $12.50. Always an alteration that could be passed off as an honest mistake, a benign slip of the finger, and just a little bit each day. They did not want to bum rush the accountants with big figures, at least not just yet. Next, they waited to see if their little ripple would make it to shore. To make a long story short it did, but it was no longer a ripple. It was full blown tidal wave of well deserved payback!

This approach works well in a seasonal setting, like the National Park circuit, which has a steady barrage of tour buses, lots of fresh, confused faces in all departments, and the inevitable chaos that goes along with that.

Data Entry Scams: Any time you enter a number into the system that is erroneous, to your benefit, and it goes through, you have pulled off a Data Entry Scam. It may be as simple as punching in under the wrong pay code, as a bartender instead of a waiter, picking up 2 or 3 extra bucks an hour or as big as the voucher scam described above. It is hard not to overfish your sleepy bean counter once he starts biting, but if you play it smart, this can be a good long term payer.

Playing It Off: You might very well get caught, but doing what exactly? Slipping erroneous numbers into the computer system, sneaking them past your manager, the accounting office, the payroll office, and then again past your manager in the form of an obviously over-fat paycheck? What kind of idiot or evil genius would bother with those odds? For management to accuse you of this scam is to admit their own utter incompetence, and many will opt to keep that a secret.

19

≈ *The Finishing Touches* ≈

"It ain't over til the fat lady sings!"

The Scam: A little last minute waiter's *leger de main* as the customer is wrapping things up never hurt anybody, least of all the waiter.

The "Thank You and Thank You Again": When a restaurant adds an automatic gratuity to its checks, it is not at all uncommon for the customer to overlook it and double tip the waiter by accident. These oversights can add up fast depending on the size of the check, and are worthy of your special attention.

Diversionary Tactics: Any way that you can think of to conceal or camouflage the added gratuity will increase your chances here.

-Smear the gratuity stamp as a matter of course, with the object of rendering the details of the check illegible and generating a higher percentage of oblivious tippers.

-Write or circle the final total in some grandiose fashion or inscribe a tearful goodbye, so as to slightly cover or confuse the totals. "Have a great trip!" "Thank you, thank you!"

-Write the final total on the back of the check and serve it backside up with peppermints.

-If you are working the bar, giving an all inclusive verbal total without even presenting the check for perusal is a sure fire way to double whack'em.

Hiding the Tip in the Total: The typical drill, when someone pays with a credit card and gratuity has been included is to enter the tip so that it appears on the "tip" line where the customer would normally write it in, so that there is no confusion. The waiter-in-the-know, however...

1. Adds the dinner total and the included gratuity together and enters that amount on the first line as if it were the dinner total only.

2. Leaves the tip slot and the final total slot open.

3. Allows the sleepy customer to add yet another tip and total it out himself.

"I Got You Anyway, Sucka'!" When a tight diner decides to stiff you on a credit card and is stupid enough to leave himself open, hit him where it counts!

1. **The Blank Check:** If the bashful guest does not think you have the rocks to fill it out yourself and leaves the signed slip without the tip or the final total, he is making a big mistake. We have seen some waiters go crazy on this, but it is best to stay between 15 and 35 percent so that the cheap bastard will not contest it with his or her credit card company.

2. **The Artist:** If you have an eye for detail, carefully changing a four to an eight, or adding a one or zero here and there can more than make up for that slap in the face.

Padding the Ticket: When you are waiting on a party of six or more, and one person is picking up the tab, beef up the automatic 15% gratuity by throwing on extra drinks or small food items as you are tallying up the final check. More often than not, the group leader will want to play it cool and will magnanimously hand over his card without closely reviewing the bill.

"Oops! Wrong Check!": (see Chapter 14)

Playing It Off: Always use discretion with those scams that involve credit cards. Poor ol' Schmoo is not always as dumb as she looks, and given enough contested transactions, might actually take the form of a restaurant manager.

20

⚞ The Wagonwheel ⚟

**"If rape is the order of the day, then rape I will,
and with a vengeance."
- Henry Miller**

The Scam: Well, well, well...what a little pack of monsters we've created. We couldn't be more proud. Huddle up boys and girls and pay close attention; this last one has some finer details to consider.

Breakthroughs in computer manipulation ring in a new and exciting era of sophistication for the art of Scam, a sophistication that represents huge financial gains to those of you still living in the past, but willing to study up. Almost all restaurant computer systems have the capacity to organize a single table's order into separate checks at the customer's request, facilitating separate payments. This is done by splitting the table into different seat numbers, moving food from the original seat to the newly created seats, in whatever groupings you need, and printing out a separate check for each seat.

For example, you have a three top that wants separate checks, and their entire order is as follows:

3 Bahama Mama Cocktails, 2 Bud lights, 3 cups of Soup du Jour, a Ribeye steak, a Crawfish Etouffee, and a Pasta Primavera.

On your computer, when you first ring it in, this food is all on Seat One, and looks something like this (Figure 1.1):

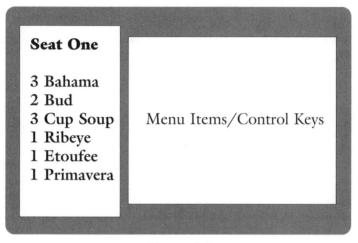

Figure 1.1

Once you initiate the Separate Check Function, it will give you the option of adding however many seats you need, in this case three (Figure 1.2):

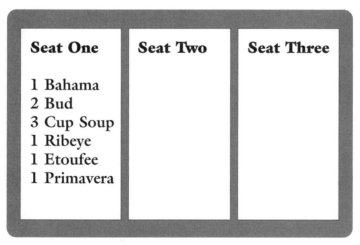

Figure 1.2

Now you are free to move items to their respective seats. How this is done is a little different from one machine to another. On Touch-Screen systems you simply touch the item you want to move, and then touch the area where you want it to wind up and it appears there. On others, you might have to select the item somehow, and transfer it by a series of keystrokes. Either way it is easily done, and in the end the items are divided as per the customer's instructions, like so (Figure 1.3):

Seat One	Seat Two	Seat Three
1 Bahama	1 Bahama	1 Bahama
1 Cup Soup	1 Cup Soup	2 Bud
1 Ribeye	1 Etoufee	1 Cup Soup
		1 Primavera

Figure 1.3

At this point you may print out all or some of the separate checks as you need them, and that is the extent of the function's legal application.

What makes the Wagonwheel possible is that you are able to move all the items back to the original seat or back and forth between whatever seats you like, in whatever groupings you desire, printing out tickets of the various combinations whenever you need to, as many times as you want! Whoops!

How to Burn Down the House

Now, with all that in mind, let's explore the two major applications of the Wagonwheel. In both of the following scenarios, we will assume that you work in a situation where you have easy access to the bar, either via a dirty bartender (see Chapter 13), or because you make your own drinks. We will also assume the availability of the usual self serve items, like soups and salads (see Chapter 9).

Wagonwheeling Separate Checks on the Same Table: Let's take another look at the above table. They still want separate checks, but *before you ring any food or drinks into the computer,* look at what each individual is ordering and note what each order has in common. In this case, each guest has ordered one Bahama Mama and one Soup du Jour.

Guest One	Guest Two	Guest Three
1 Bahama Mama	1 Bahama Mama	1 Bahama Mama
1 Soup du Jour	1 Soup du Jour	2 Bud Lights
1 Ribeye Steak	1 Etouffee	1 Soup du Jour
		1 Pasta Primavera

The neanderthal waiter sees some good sales and maybe a good tip if he grovels enthusiastically enough, with a pain-in-the-ass separate check table to boot. The liberated waiter sees a field of diamonds. The former has another long night ahead of him, while the latter endorses this cheerful approach.

1. Ring in all of the food, but rather than ringing in three Bahama Mamas and three Soup du Jours, *only ring in one of each.*

2. Initiate the Separate Check Function and separate the bill into three different seats, leaving the Bahama Mama and the Soup du Jour on Seat One. It should look something like this (Figure 2.1):

75

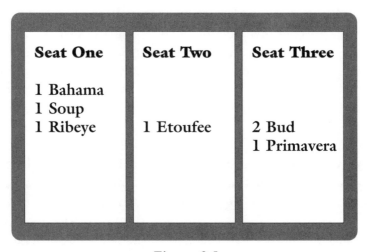

Figure 2.1

3. Print a check for Seat One and save it.

4. Select the Bahama Mama and the Soup du Jour and transfer them to Seat Two (Figure 2.2):

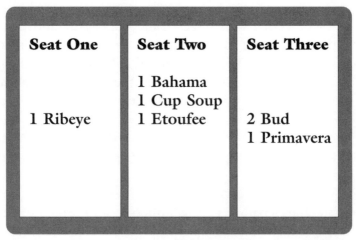

Figure 2.2

5. Print a check for Seat Two and save it.

6. Select the Bahama Mama and Soup du Jour again, and transfer them to Seat Three (Figure 2.3):

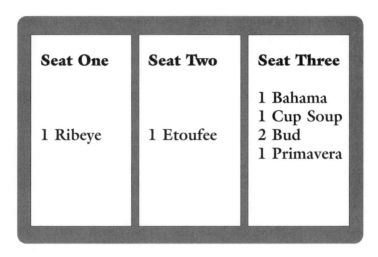

Seat One	Seat Two	Seat Three
1 Ribeye	1 Etoufee	1 Bahama 1 Cup Soup 2 Bud 1 Primavera

Figure 2.3

7. Print a check for Seat Three and save it. You now have these three printed checks that account for three Bahama mamas and three Soup du Jours:

Seat One	Seat Two	Seat Three
1 Bahama Mama	1 Bahama Mama	1 Bahama Mama
1 Soup du Jour	1 Soup du Jour	2 Bud Lights
1 Ribeye Steak	1 Etouffee	1 Soup du Jour
		1 Pasta Primavera

But you have only rung in one Bahama Mama and one Soup du Jour. You feel me?

8. Serve the checks and collect. You are left with a cash difference of two Bahama Mamas and two Soup du Jours.

As you can see, all three checks revolve around the same drink and soup, the way spokes revolve around the hub of a wheel, and that is how this scam picked up its curious moniker (Figure 3.1):

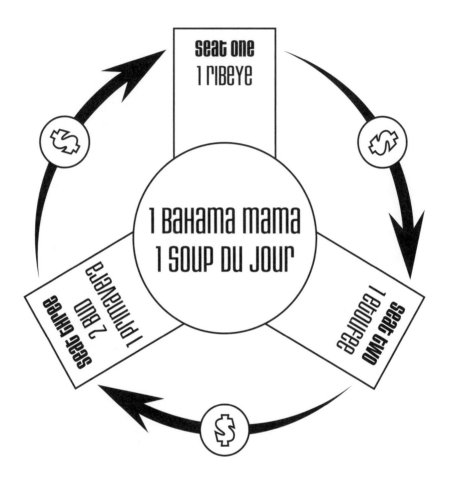

Figure 3.1 "The Wagonwheel"

Wagonwheeling Separate Tables: Although the circumstances are different, the mechanics of the Wagonwheel's second application are identical to the first. This scenario involves scamming the common items of two or more completely different tables. We will use the following two tables as an example:

Table 21	Table 13
2 Budweiser	1 Budweiser
2 House Salad	1 House Salad
2 Blackened Redfish	1 Jerk Chicken Salad

1   Table 21 arrives first. Take their order and enter it in the computer.

2. Table 13 arrives shortly thereafter. You take their order, *but do not ring it in just yet.*

3. Just like before, take a moment to note the common items between the two orders, in this case: 1 Budweiser and 1 House Salad. These represent the hub of your Wagonwheel.

4. Rather than initiating a whole new check for Table 13, subtract the items that it has in common with Table 21 (1 Bud and 1 House Salad) and ring the remainder (1 Jerk Chicken Salad) on Table 21's already existing check. Now Table 21 and Table 13 are combined on one check, and it should look like this on the computer screen (Figure 4.1):

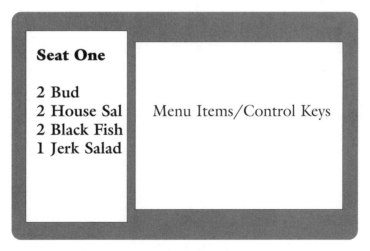

Figure 4.1

5. From here on out we proceed as if we were Wagon-wheeling Separate Checks. Just like before, add one seat using the Separate Check or comparable function (Figure 4.2):

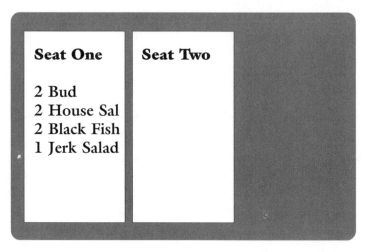

Figure 4.2

6. Select the items that need to appear on the check for Table 13 (1 Bud, 1 House Salad, and 1 Jerk Chicken Salad) and move them to Seat Two (Figure 4.3):

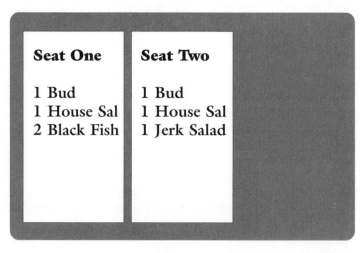

Figure 4.3

7. Print the check for Seat Two/Table 13 and save it.

8. Select the items from Seat Two that need to appear on Table 21's check (1 Bud and 1 House Salad) and move them back to Seat One (figure 4.4):

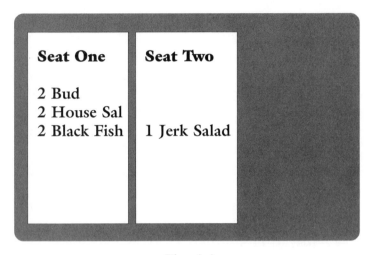

Fig. 4.4

9. Print the check for Seat One/Table 21 and save it. You now have these two printed checks that account for 3 Budweisers and 3 House Salads, but you have only rung in 2 Budweisers and 2 House Salads, no?

Table 21	Table 13
2 Budweiser	1 Budweiser
2 House Salad	1 House Salad
2 Blackened Redfish	1 Jerk Chicken Salad

10. Serve the checks and collect. You are left with a cash difference of 1 Budweiser and 1 House Salad. This is a modest, if not meager profit considering the technology at work here, but we have kept things as simple as possible for the sake of comprehension. Once you take your training wheels off, this baby is a real steamroller.

This completes Wagonwheel 101: Basic Rotational Theory. In the following section, we will introduce some simple techniques that will increase your rpm, and touch on a few ways to keep your fat out of the fire.

The Carrion Check: Despite all its fancy printouts and glistening silicon circuitry, the Wagonwheel, like any other scam, only works with cash payments. There are ways to strong-arm the customer into paying cash, like Putting Them on Ice (see Chapter 5), but there is never any guarantee, and all too often, all your hard work and preparation is shot to hell by a blasted credit card. However, there is one way to plan ahead for plastic.

For one reason or another not all cash checks are incorporated into some kind of scam. Either the circumstances do not allow it, or you have already hosed the place down for a conspicuous amount and are trying accrue a legitimate amount of cash transactions to balance things out. At any rate, in the case that you are left with a big, seemingly useless, cash check, *do not close it out,* that is: do not finalize the transaction in the computer so that you no longer have access to it. Here is why.

Let's pretend that you have a seventy dollar table, they eat, pay cash, and leave. You play it smart and do not close out the ticket. Around the same time you have another table with two dozen oysters and two iced teas: items that you managed to get yourself, without submitting a ticket. Their bill is twenty dollars, and you are looking forward to a little free money, but dagnabbit! They pull out a credit card right at the last minute! Not to worry:

1. Pull up the old seventy dollar cash check.

2. Apply the new twenty dollar credit card payment to that check.

3. In this way you seamlessly displace twenty dollars from its old position on the *unused* cash check, to its new position in your pocket.

4. The customer doesn't care, so long as he receives a credit card receipt that matches the total you quoted him.

If the old cash check is big enough you can use it a few times, taking tasty chunks out of it with different credit cards as you see fit.

Don't Be Too Specific. Use general headings to account for items whenever possible. In other words, if a table orders a Bud Light, ring it in as a plain ol' Bud. That way if another table comes into the picture and orders a plain ol' Bud, you can incorporate them into a given scam without raising any eyebrows. The first customer will assume that all Bud products are rung under the same heading, if he thinks anything at all. However, if you were to play it by the book, and ring in the original Bud Light as a Bud Light, and then try to pass that off as a plain ol' Bud, the second *rube* customer would, at the very least, realize that you rang up his beer incorrectly. The same goes for everything. If you are responsible for making all of a variety of salads, say, regular House Salads, Caesar Salads, and Spinach Salads; ring everything under "House Salad".

Think Before You Close Out Your Checks. There is no reason to reduce your options unless you absolutely have to. If you have a check with some popular, easy-access items that are bound to pop up again soon; leave it open, or leave a big cash check open to be used as a Carrion Check.

When to Spin the Wheel: The safest time to use the wagon wheel is in the case of *Wagonwheeling Separate Checks,* as described above. It involves only one table, and upon examination appears to be a regular old check, that is, everything has been ordered at the same time and all entrees are going to the same table number.

As for *Wagonwheeling Separate Tables,* there are two possible scenarios. In the first there are two or more tables that are eating simultaneously. Although one may have come in a little bit before the other, they are both in the restaurant at the same time, and their two separate orders are combined on one check. This could be dangerous if PricknBalls realizes that the two kitchen copies have the same table number, but sees the food go out to two or more separate tables.

In the second possible scenario, a table has eaten, paid, and left and you are spinning a new table off a couple of items from their old check. At a cursory glance everything seems to be on the up and up: one table number and one group of diners.

The Frankenstein Check: Some people make the mistake of spinning off the same check all night long. What results is a freakish patchwork check that is curiously high dollar (especially if your section has only small tables), and exhibits the suspicious, successive pattern: drinks, appetizers, entrees, drinks, appetizers, entrees, etc. *Wagonwheel one or two times at the most off any given check to avoid these incriminating mutations!*

Playing It Off: The Wagonwheel flies under the dim radar of even the most capable FloorDick, and redoubles its pleasurability quotient when executed under the nose of the same tragic character. Just try to keep that big, fat smile off your face, and once in a while complain about what bad tippers you've been cursed with, and how being a waiter really sucks. No one likes to hear about other people's problems and you'll be duly ignored. Other than that, there is only the small matter of the occasional commission check that we expect for so graciously passing along this sizable golden nugget. Be sure you write legibly, and send all donations to:

Two Bourbon Street Waiters
c/o The Mouth-Watering Cocktail Waitress
A White Sandy Beach
Rio De Janeiro, Brazil

❦ *Epilogue* ❦

Some of our readers will surely pick up a few useful tricks
from this quirky, sentimental handbook, while others may
simply nod their heads knowingly and laugh. Others still,
may not laugh at all, and who can blame them?
To all our new-found friends and enemies...

Bon Appétit!

Glossary

～❧ *Glossary* ❧～

Benjamins- Funds

Bon Appétit- Enjoy your Meal!

Comp- To discount or void all or a portion of a bill.

Credit Card Terminal- Small computer terminal/modem that verifies customer credit cards and organizes transactions under different server numbers.

Dine and Dasher- Someone who walks out without paying his or her bill.

86- To stop serving an item for one reason or another.

Employee of the Month- Scamming waiter flying below the radar of the house management.

FloorDick- Restaurant manager, owner, or any authority figure on the job.

Good Samaritan- Manager with a soft spot for workers, easily manipulated.

Gratuity- Tip

Gratuity Stamp- Rubber ink stamp used to indicate the gratuity on a check.

Handwritten Check- Either a scam check, fabricated by a waiter to appear legitimate, or a classic restaurant check used in a situation where no computer system is in place.

Hard Copy- The thin, bottom, cardboard copy of a two or three part carbon-paper guest check.

House- Restaurant or bar.

In the Weeds- Extremely busy.

Leger De Main- Slight of hand.

Loose Cannon- Reckless, turned-out manager lacking self control.

Manna- Food miraculously supplied to the Israelites. A sudden and unforeseen source of gratification.

Meal Voucher- Ticket provided to a tourist or hotel guest as part of their tour package that can be exchanged for food and/or drink.

Mongo- From Mongoloid. Refers to a manager with the IQ of a retarded person, but without any of the corresponding flair or redemptive qualities.

The Mope- Restaurant manager, conveys a sense of self-loathing, pointlessness.

Phantom Drinks- Extra drinks added to a bar tab without the knowledge of the customer, either to beef up the gratuity or just for spite.

Pick-up Window- Window-like aperture wherein the cooks place completed entrees and appetizers to be picked up by the waiters.

PricknBalls- Rare and menacing manager with a shred of competency.

Pump Handle- Name given to truly talented and accomplished scam artists.

Recycled Check- A check that is used more than once by a scamming waiter or bartender.

Ring In- To enter an order into the computer or cash register.

Schmoo- Oddly-shaped, groveling restaurant manager.

Scamster- Waiter or bartender well-versed in the art of hoodwinking managers and guests out of monies.

Seasonal Gig- A job that only lasts a portion of the year, e.g.- a summer job at a national park, a winter job at a ski resort, etc.

Self-Service Items- Items, such as salads, soup, iced tea, etc., that a waiter can get his hands on without submitting a corresponding ticket.

Server Number- A number assigned to a waiter or bartender used to identify him in the electronic systems of a restaurant or bar.

Short-Changed Super- Oblivious manager.

Stiff- To screw a waiter or bartender out of his tip.

Three Top- A table with three people. Also, two top, four top, five top, etc.

Top Shelf- Expensive, name-brand liquors.

Verbal Check- When a waiter or bartender verbally quotes a price to a customer, without serving an itemized paper check.

Void- To remove an item or items from a computerized ticket. This must be performed by a manager with a secret password or code key.

Walk-Out- When a diner leaves secretly, without paying his or her bill.

Well Liquor- Cheaply bought liquor that the House serves to customers who do not specify a particular brand, or for drink specials.

Who are Peter Francis and R.Chip DeGlinkta?

The unlikely and colorful vanguards of Promethean Books' new publishing venture are not your everyday writers. In fact, some say that they have been obliged to don the cruel yoke of literacy out of the sheer originality and social relevence of their mutual experiences. Years of travel and free-wheeling adventures have seasoned the duo with an air of worldliness and wisdom that can only be achieved after many successes and many more failures. Readers will find an earthy camaraderie in their tone and a welcome absence of sanctimony or condescension. Despite their recent critical success, these two "street-toughened working boys" have not forgotten their humble roots.

Ironically, they met on stage in the early nineties as the Dauphin and the Duke of Bridgewater in a rare performance of Mark Twain's *Huckleberry Finn,* roles that closely parallel their own hurly-burly existence and rambunctious but lovable personalities. The two have always shared a fascination with the chicanery and confabulation that is so characteristic of the enigmatic human animal. For years now, they have navigated the uncharted nether regions of American society where these antics are commonplace, seeking out the elusive Scam Masters and imploring their invaluable tutelage. The quest, while ongoing, has been an unquestionable success, and at last, their carefully tended tree of taboo knowledge has borne its first delicious fruit. *How to Burn Down the House: The Infamous Waiter and Bartender's Scam Bible* is the result of tireless research: bartending, waiting tables, and relentlessly shearing the unwitting, drunken folds of New Orleans' notorious Bourbon Street.

The *Scam Bible* is merely the first installment of Promethean Books' *In the Know Series,* the ongoing documentation of the eye-opening discoveries of Francis and DeGlinkta, America's most controversial and self-educated anthropologists. Be sure to check out *scambible.com,* a wellspring of scam insight hosted by the authors, where inquiring minds can query the two scam masters via *Ask the Scam Oracle,* or share an original scam that they may have witnessed or participated in themselves. Either way, check in regularly for the newest angles on this greatest of American pastimes...Enterprising Freely!

About Promethean Books

Promethean Books, originally named The Promethean Press, was formed in 1996 by New Orleans poet and writer, John F. Collins. The Promethean Press, like many small presses across America, was an optimistic, perhaps idealistic, community-based effort focused on providing a creative forum for New Orleans writing and writers.

By sponsoring the New Orleans Literary Renaissance Project, a series of local writing contests and eclectic readings, The Promethean Press was able to stimulate an ongoing literary interface between writer and reader: one still going strong today. It became clear that the potential of local talent, as yet untapped, was abundant and rich.

Finally, in collaboration with *Tribe Magazine,* The Eisenhower Center, and *Rant for the Renaissance,* an unprecedented convergence known as the *Insomniacathon: Voices Without Restraint* took place. Beat luminaries like Robert Creeley, William S.Burroughs, Allen Ginsberg, Diane DiPrima, Gregory Corso, Lawrence Ferlinghetti, and countless others came together to amalgamate and anoint their legacies. Contemporary New Orleans writers and poets helped take the torch from a fading generation and re-ignite it to luminate the future and beyond.

In time, Collins teamed up with Austin, Texas artist and writer, Nigel Pickhardt, and the two formed the present collaboration, Promethean Books. This exciting publishing venture is bent on shining a bright light into those infinite recesses of the Human Condition, mining the ore of the written word.

Look for these thought-provoking titles
coming soon from Promethean Books:

THE INTERROGATION OF CHE GUEVARA: A PLAY.
By John F.Collins
Copyright ©2004 Promethean Books

This unique piece embarks from the supposition that the Latin-American revolutionary hero and sixties counter-cultural icon, Che Guevara, was not in fact murdered by the Bolivian Government and the CIA in 1967 as history implies, but rather that he was kept alive and interrogated by his captors. This surprising and powerful play explores the motivations, justifications, and damnations of the great Latin-American Marxist Revolution.

POIA
By John F.Collins and Micheal Rihner
Copyright ©2004 Promethean Books

In 1910, the only known Native-American opera was written, and later performed in Berlin, Germany. It was an original interpretation of the Blackfeet Christ story, *Poia*. In 2001 Collins and Rihner undertook to write a new rendition with a folk twist. The result is an amalgam of Native-American mythology and western Christianity that is compelling and thoroughly uplifting.

THE STONER'S COOKBOOK
By Peter Francis and R.Chip DeGlinkta
Copyright ©2004 Promethean Books

Peter Francis and R.C.DeGlinkta, those light-hearted ambassadors of the underworld, are back...with the cookbook for the cooked! Jam-packed with lip-smacking recipes and invaluable culinary insight for the stoners among us, not to mention heaping bowlfuls of all the hilarity one might expect to find when the munchies are mixed with hot ovens. You can smell the smoke from here!

Give *How to Burn Down the House* to Friends, Family, and Colleagues Today! Check Your Local Bookstore or Order Here.

☐ Yes, I want _____ copies of *How to Burn Down the House: The Infamous Waiter & Bartender's Scam Bible* for $12.95 each.

☐ Yes, I am interested in having Peter Francis and R.Chip DeGlinkta speak or give a seminar to my company, school, or organization. Send me information.

Include $3.95 Shipping and Handling for one book and add $1.95 extra for each additional book. Louisiana residents must include 4% State Sales Tax. New Orleans residents add an additional 5% City Tax (9% total). Canadian orders must include payments in US funds, with 7% GST added.

Payment must accompany orders. Allow 3 weeks for delivery.

My Check or Money Order for $_____ is Enclosed.
Please Charge My: ☐ Visa   ☐ Mastercard
☐ American Express   ☐ Discover

Name_____

Organization_____

Address _____

City/State/Zip _____

Phone _____E-Mail _____

Credit Card #_____

Expiration Date _____Signature _____

Call (888)672-9018
Make Your Check Payable and Return to:
Promethean Books
1000 Bourbon Street #250
New Orleans, La
70119

www.prometheanbooks.com / www.scambible.com